BECOME A JUNIOR ENTREPRENEUR

VRUNDA BANSODE

Foreword by Anuradha Kedia and Dhimant Parekh, Founders, The Better India

illustrations by MEGHNA MENON

PUFFIN BOOKS

An imprint of Penguin Random House

PUFFIN BOOKS

USA | Canada | UK | Ireland | Australia
New Zealand | India | South Africa | China | Singapore

Puffin Books is part of the Penguin Random House group of companies
whose addresses can be found at global.penguinrandomhouse.com

Published by Penguin Random House India Pvt. Ltd.
4th Floor, Capital Tower 1, MG Road,
Gurugram 122 002, Haryana, India

Penguin
Random House
India

First published in Puffin Books by Penguin Random House India 2020

Text copyright © Vrunda Bansode 2020
Illustrations copyright © Meghna Menon 2020

ISBN 9780143445975

Typeset in Adobe Garamond Pro by Manipal Technologies Limited, Manipal
Book design and layout by Devangana Dash and Meghna Menon
Printed at Replika Press Pvt. Ltd, India

www.penguin.co.in

MIX
Paper | Supporting
responsible forestry
FSC™ C016779

CONTENTS

CONTENTS

FOREWORD: WORDS OF ENCOURAGEMENT

This foreword is written by two people, and we'll save you the trouble of waiting till the end to know our names. We are Anuradha and Dhimant, founders of The Better India.

Growing up in Bangalore, we were always told that there was only one path to success—become an engineer and get a job at a good company. So, we did what we were told. Anuradha became a civil engineer and Dhimant became a computer science engineer. We both started our working lives with two large technology companies.

And that would have remained our path if we had not, by chance, met some entrepreneurs at business school. For the first time, we realized that you could indeed build your own company, run your own business and pursue dreams that were not confined to the traditional idea of a job.

We distinctly remember the day our idea took shape. It was a fine sunny day, almost a year after we had graduated from business school. We sat down with our morning cup of tea and picked up the newspaper. The front page was full of crime news and scandals that revealed the bleak state of affairs in the country. It just left us feeling disappointed and full of despair. We didn't quite understand why there was so much coverage of all the terrible things and why no one, absolutely no one, was talking about all the good things happening around us. Every single day, the newspaper was bringing gloom right into our living rooms.

This disproportionate coverage of the negative didn't seem right. We decided to read and learn more about all the progressive acts happening in the country, but we couldn't find a single platform that covered such news. Finally, we decided to build it ourselves. We strongly believed (and still do) that it is only when you inspire people that you see a massive change in our communities. And thus was born The Better India, which we worked on as a side project while we continued our day jobs.

We would go around the city on weekends, documenting and photographing people doing some truly impactful work. Slowly, friends and family started reading these stories and they started sharing them with their circle of friends. A network was being built and, more importantly, our stories were changing lives!

With almost every story we wrote, there would be a feedback email telling us how that story changed someone's life or perception. We were influencing mindsets and driving people to make a difference. And that gave us courage and fuel to do more.

So, we persisted. We kept writing stories almost every single day while juggling our personal lives, day jobs and keeping this platform alive. And then we did the unthinkable—we quit our jobs and dived right into growing The Better India. Most people at that time, including our family, felt that we had lost the plot. Here were two engineers, with B-school degrees from one of the most prestigious business schools in the country, jeopardizing their lucrative careers.

But we didn't let that deter us from our single vision—we wanted to build a business that would have massive impact at a large scale. We dug deep into our savings and gave it our all—and eventually, the persistence started to pay off.

More people started reading The Better India, advertisers started to take note of us and we started touching hundreds of thousands of lives for the better. What kept us going? That single-minded focus on creating impact and building scale. We always ensured that the larger goal was in front of us, driving us on.

What we lacked during that entire period is a guide, or a resource centre of sorts. We literally had to build our own rules, by trial and error or based on our own instinctive judgements.

However, that should not be the case for our future entrepreneurs—the kids who are growing up with so many dreams and ideas. There is no reason why every entrepreneur should reinvent the wheel every single time. There are some basic tenets that can be made available for all—this truly helps further the ecosystem of entrepreneurship.

Which brings us to this book and why it is so important for all of us to read it. With the wide gamut of opportunities now available to our children, all that's lacking is a structured approach and a method to their madness. Our eleven-year-old is smitten with entrepreneurial visions (perhaps a result of hearing both of his parents discuss business all day), but where he needs help is in understanding the basics.

This is exactly why we were excited to learn about Vrunda's book. If there's one person who can do justice to a topic like this, it's Vrunda with her wide experience with modern teaching methodologies and by being deeply involved with entrepreneurship at IIM Bangalore. If you have the passion to change something around you, this book gives you the necessary indicators that will enable you to start your journey. It has examples that you can relate to, it has learnings from various scenarios that you will find extremely useful.

Above all, it's a great window into the beautiful world of entrepreneurship. Dive right in.

Anuradha Kedia
Dhimant Parekh
Founders, The Better India
and The Better Home

A NOTE FROM THE AUTHOR

What if every teenager got a chance to be an entrepreneur? What if everyone got an opportunity to experience the thrill of launching a venture, thinking of ideas, trying out ways of doing better, solving problems at every stage—and earning money at the age of sixteen? Will it change their outlook towards responsibility, learning and work?

As part of the experiential education by Cloud Mentor, a venture I was part of, we ran a programme for eleventh grade commerce students called Entrepreneurship Lab at a school in Bangalore. In five years, this in-depth entrepreneurship experience touched close to 200 students.

What all did this experience include?

a. **Staying with them as a mentor and guide:** We realized that entrepreneurship is a journey that cannot be hastened. It comes from within and every student finds it at their own pace. So, we devised this as a year-long programme that included weekly sessions.

b. **Helping them learn to work in unfamiliar teams:** Every year, we followed a conscious policy of us deciding how to divide the class of 35–40 into groups of 5–7 students each. We considered multiple factors, such as proximity of residences and gender balance, in each group. In real life, workplaces and teams are not always made up of people you are already friends with—you build good relationships with them while working. We wanted students to experience this and ensured that they worked in their assigned teams despite their pleas, pleadings, threats and tears because their best friends were in other teams. By the end of every year, these teams invariably became best buddies and discovered new talents, matching interests and respect for each other within their groups.

c. **No teaching and no making decisions for them:** Except for a very basic explanation of important concepts, we never really taught any theory. Theory, after all, emerges out of practice. We shared stories of lots and lots of businesses and start-ups. We let them research brands of their interest and encouraged them to talk to their seniors and learn from their experiences. We let the students find their own role models and discover unique business strategies that resonated with them.

d. **Managing the resources:** We put a strict cap on the money the students were allowed to borrow from their parents to start the business because which entrepreneur gets easy capital in the real world? So, what did this constraint do for them? Put a dampener on their enthusiasm? Far from it! It made them strive, innovate and do wonders! For example, one group very opportunistically made merchandise overnight, using the school colours, to sell on Sports Day at 100 per cent profit. This helped them collect more capital to infuse into their main business of cr-eat-ive nachos!

e. **Not helping, but enabling them to succeed:** There was never a push, a clampdown or disciplinary action ever taken in this class, but there was always a nudge to be well organized, well prepared, creative and yet focused on the outcome. Each assignment had a tangible outcome that enabled the teams to take decisions and move on to the next steps. For example, a group was torn between which cupcakes to bake—strawberry or chocolate. They designed their own market survey questionnaire, collected answers and decided to go with chocolate because

90 per cent of their target customers wanted it! We never gave them a quick decision; they figured it out themselves.

f. **Taking 'failure' out of their vocabulary:** Experiments were the only teachers in this class. Some groups did not make as much money as they had hoped, while some products did not pan out according to the expectations. Each such episode was merely a pointer to a change in the right direction. The more such pointers you collect, the wiser you become! Failing does not make one a failure, being afraid of failing does.

So what did this experience do for those students? Each year, we had a 'Graduation Day' where each group summarized their experiences and business results, which they presented to their parents. The heart-warming words we most commonly heard were:

a. **I learnt to make decisions:** Throughout all my school years, we were taught and asked to understand. Here, we had to figure out what we wanted to do, why we wanted to do it and how! It was scary at first but eventually immensely satisfying to do what we thought was right.

b. **I understood responsibility and ownership:** Staying up till 4 a.m. baking cupcakes and weaving loom bands, running around a large school campus carrying a boxful of things, finding the right sort of packaging material in the labyrinthine wholesale market—all because I promised my teammates that I would do it!

c. **I learnt to listen and collaborate:** This was not a competition! I had to listen to my teammates, respect their decisions, work as per the common plan and pitch in when required. I made fantastic new friends and memories to cherish forever!

d. **I am not afraid of taking a risk or trying something new:** The whole experience was about trying new things. I was so unsure at the beginning of the year—and in the end, I am proud of what we achieved! I know now that I can do anything if I put my mind to it and plan well.

e. **I understand the value of money now:** When I walked kilometres to find the cheapest vendor and found something at Rs 14 per kg, which was otherwise Rs 17 per kg, my joy knew no bounds! I never thought about how much each rupee mattered—now I know.

And did they learn how to run a business? Every concept they learnt in economics—demand, supply, market, price; everything they learnt in accounting—revenue, expenditure, break-even; all that they learnt in business studies—the four Ps of marketing, buying behaviour, market study—every single concept was put to good use!

But most importantly, it is this change that came from within that will stay with them forever, irrespective of the profession they choose. This entrepreneurial mindset is the best tool that we can arm them with to do well in the world of tomorrow.

This book captures the essence and the structure of our programme, laid out in a set of steps that can be followed, whether at home or in school with larger groups. It lets you find the entrepreneur within. I hope you find it helpful.

GETTING STARTED

Become a Junior Entrepreneur is an interactive guide that will answer your questions at whichever stage of the entrepreneurial journey you are in.

a. Read this book with your friends or in a group with whom you'd like to develop your business idea. Invite people into your process of ideation and get feedback or assistance from them. A good entrepreneur always listens.

b. Look for the pencil icon in each chapter for prompts and activities to develop your ideas! You could do these activities either on the pages of the book or in your own notebook.

c. Every entrepreneur needs to understand the world they're operating within and that starts with knowing the lingo. A **yellow line** under a word in the book indicates that it is an essential entrepreneurial term. You will find their meanings in the glossary section at the end of the book.

And remember, you'll understand the world of entrepreneurship a little better with every reading of the book.

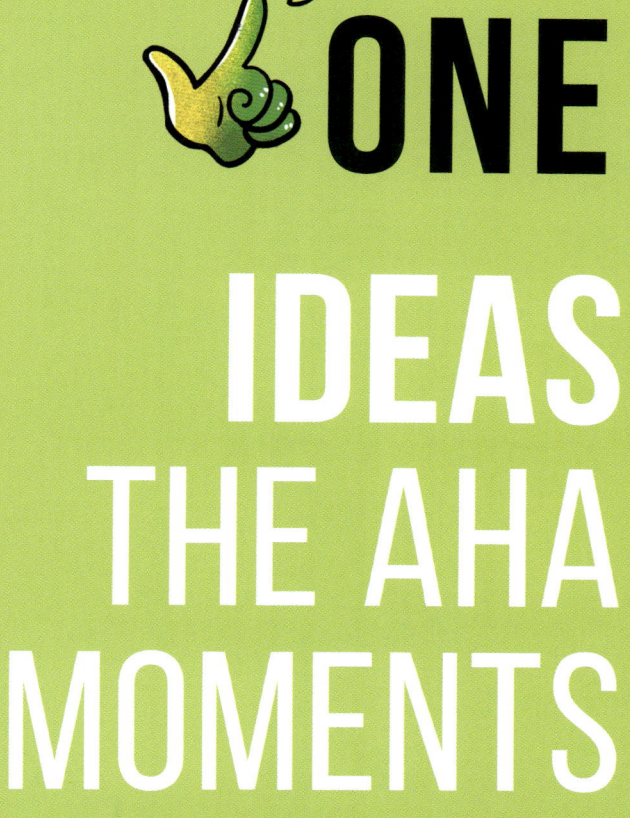

ONE

IDEAS
THE AHA
MOMENTS

A rock pile ceases to be a rock pile the moment a single man contemplates it, bearing within him the image of a cathedral.
—ANTOINE DE SAINT-EXUPÉRY, FRENCH AVIATOR AND ACCLAIMED WRITER

#1
WHO WANTS TO BE AN ENTREPRENEUR?

'What do you want to be when you grow up?'

How many times have you heard that question? If you got a hundred bucks each time you heard it, you would be a millionaire I bet! Why is everyone so obsessed with what you are going to be? What does it mean?

If you look at the world around you, what do you see? People going to work to earn money and then the same people spending that money! And of course, during your school and college years, you will repeatedly hear about the importance of working towards a good career and earning well. But why is money so important?

Just think of what you typically do in a day. All of us use multiple products and services in our daily lives. The breakfast cereal that you eat, biscuits that you munch on, soap that you bathe with, shoes that you wear, your school bag, uniform, pencils and pens—can you make do without any of these? Or your favourite TV channel, your mobile phone operator, Google,

WhatsApp—what will you do without their services? Now, all of these products and services, which make your life comfortable and happy, have been produced by other people. Most products are made by people who work in factories. These products are then shipped all over the world and sold by people who work in shops. Your favourite TV shows and songs are produced by people who work in the entertainment industry. This is what keeps our society running. People who provide these products and services get paid for doing their work. That money—the salary or the professional income that your parents get—is what your family uses to buy the food, the soap, the school supplies, the cable TV subscription, new phones and clothes. Very simply, money is what keeps the economy running, churning and working!

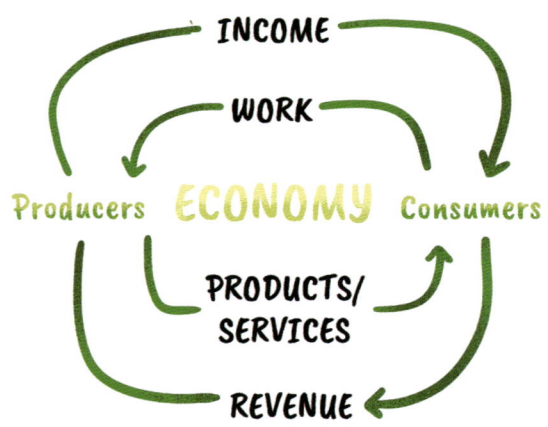

When you grow up and pursue a profession, you will earn money too. There are so many exciting options for you to choose from, depending on what you'd like to be. One of the choices you can make—which your teachers and parents don't tell you about—is to become an entrepreneur. So, who are entrepreneurs? What kind of work do they do? How do they earn money? What does becoming an entrepreneur mean?

Can you name some entrepreneurs?

....

....

....

....

....

....

....

....

....

....

How do you think Instagram came into existence? I am sure your parents have told you a number of times that when they were of your age, they didn't have Instagram or iPad games or even mobile phones! So there was someone who *made* Instagram a few years ago. (And here's a quick exercise for you: find out who founded Instagram and why.)

The people who make a new product or service available in the market for public consumption are called entrepreneurs. And so the people who started Apple, Instagram, Facebook, Swiggy, Flipkart, Paper Boat, Yoga Bar, Naturals Ice Cream, Adidas and Wildcraft are all entrepreneurs. They thought of a new product or a service that will be useful to people, then designed and developed it and started selling it in the market. Other people like you and me found these new things useful and we started buying them. And that's how businesses are built.

When a business starts getting bigger, it needs more people to help produce more, sell more and keep things in order. Businesses employ people to work as engineers, machine workers, salespeople, accountants, managers and more. When you think about it, you realize that it is the entrepreneur who creates jobs and income opportunities for other people! On one hand, an entrepreneur serves our needs by making useful things, and on the other hand, they employ other people and pay them. It is the entrepreneur who keeps the economy running.

As new, useful products and services make lives better, entrepreneurship is really important for the economy to grow and prosper.

So, how does one become an entrepreneur? Is there a degree or a course in college that you must pursue? Not at all! To work as a doctor, you need to get a degree from a medical college. It's similar for engineers and architects. But anyone can become an entrepreneur!

All you need is . . . well, now that you know what entrepreneurs do, can you think of what they need?

....

....

....

....

....

....

....

....

....

....

....

....

....

....

When your teacher teaches you a new maths concept and gives some problems to solve, typically she'll also teach you a step-by-step method to solve them. You then follow the steps and get the right answer. But what if she never taught you the steps and merely said, 'Find out the amount of paint and money you will need to paint the entire interior area of your house'? How will you go about solving this problem?

You will have to think of an approach; try something out on your own. You will need to do research. You might need to talk to some people. You might have to change your approach. You might be somewhat right, somewhat wrong!

And that's how it is with entrepreneurship. When you are creating a new product and a new business, there are no specific steps to follow. It is up to you. It is entirely your creation as an entrepreneur. You get to decide how it should look, its name, its price, what it should and should not do. Will it work? Will people like it? There are no easy or quick answers. You will have to think, try it out, research, talk to people and be ready to change tack. And you will always be somewhat right and somewhat wrong.

What are the qualities that an entrepreneur should possess?

 **a. Thinking:** There are no steps to follow, so think of your own.

 **b. Innovation:** You are making a NEW thing.

 c. Risk-taking: It's a new path; you never know what you might encounter.

 **d. People skills:** You need a happy team and a lot of happy **customers**.

 **e. Business skills:** Know your product and your customers; develop a sense of how to use your money.

 **f. Hard work:** Being an entrepreneur is a 24/7 job.

 **g. Humility:** Customer is king. Be willing to learn from the people around you.

#2
IDEAS IDEAS IDEAS

What kind of things do entrepreneurs make and build their businesses around? Let us think.

A company like Tata Motors makes cars. A car is a physical product that we can see, touch, feel and use. A car is a mode of transport, which we use to travel from one place to another. And that is why it has an engine and wheels and a body, and that's what the car company manufactures and sells. When we buy a car, we pay to own it. It is a PRODUCT.

Now, what about Uber and Ola? We don't purchase the vehicle that they send. We merely pay the cab fare for the trip but don't own the cab. It is a SERVICE.

When we order a Domino's pizza at an outlet, we receive a physical product. When we order a Domino's pizza using the Zomato app, Zomato provides us a delivery service by delivering that product to our doorsteps.

When you go for a haircut, a stylist or a barber provides a service. When you buy new clothes, you are buying products. When you make a call, you are using

a mobile phone, a product made by multinational **brands**, such as Apple or Samsung, and using the service provided by your operator, such as Airtel or Jio.

These are all examples of companies that were started by entrepreneurs who had an IDEA for a product or a service. To create something, to make something, to sell something.

Sometimes entrepreneurs invent a completely new product, for example, Thomas Edison invented the electric light bulb and sold it through his company that we know as General Electric. Sometimes it is not a completely new product or a service but a new and better version of the old one. For example, Swiggy has not invented any new food or even the idea of getting something home delivered. But they introduced a mobile phone app that makes it easy for you to scroll through the menus of multiple restaurants, order the dish of your choice, make a quick online payment and get the food delivered to your doorstep within minutes. It is a great service innovation that has brought many benefits to its customers, producers and the delivery partners working with them.

Innovation is a continuous cycle of thinking differently and improving existing products and services. Invention is thinking of something that doesn't exist yet and then making it.

So if you could be an entrepreneur today, what will you make and sell?

What are you good at? What gets you excited? Write down your interests, skills, hobbies and passions. Also carefully observe the needs people have and the things they want. What can make their lives better, easier, more comfortable and joyful?

If you like coding and are good at design,
you could offer web design services.

If you like cooking and baking, you could start
a baking business from your home.

If you are an awesome photographer, you could start a business
making and selling photo posters or doing candid photography.

If you are a popular entertainer and enjoy parties,
you could try your hand at party planning.

If you have a great eye for fashion,
you could open your own boutique.

If you are good at making knick-knacks, you could start
a business selling handmade gifts.

14

Think of all the things that you can build on to develop your business as an entrepreneur and note them down here. Right now, do not think of constraints. Just think of all that you would like to do. Innovate. Invent. Dream big!

....
....
....
....
....
....
....
....
....
....
....
....
....

Now comes the reality check. Let us think of what you can actually work towards and have a good chance of succeeding at. How does one figure that out? Try to answer these questions for each of the businesses you have listed:

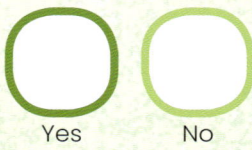

Yes   No

a. Do I myself have the skill of making this product or delivering this service?
(**Hint:** If you want to start a baking business but do not know how to bake, the answer would be No.
If you want to start a web design service and are good at using design softwares yourself, your answer is Yes.)

Yes   No

b. Do I know who might be the customers for my business and can I reach them easily?
(**Hint:** If you are developing a book-trading app and know that many of your friends will use the service, your answer is Yes. But let's say you are considering starting a garden clean-up service and don't have any houses with gardens around you, the answer is No.)

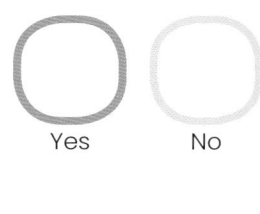

c. Do many people need this product or service?

(**Hint:** Everybody needs and buys toothbrushes regularly, so the market is large. But not everyone needs dental braces, so the market is much smaller.)

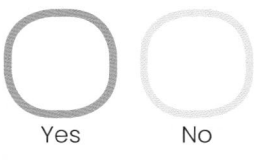

d. Roughly how much money is needed to start this business and will I be able to get it through my savings, allowances and borrowings from family and friends?

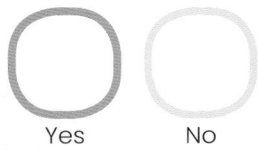

e. Can I start working towards this right away—at least within a few months?

For any idea that you end up with more No-s than Yes-es, mark it as a passion to be pursued later.

Where your Yes-es are more than the No-s, get going! If you have a Yes for all five questions, that's a great place to start. But if you had to scrap all of your ideas, don't be hassled. Just start again or see if you can modify an idea you like a little until you get all five Yes-es.

Another great way to start is to team up with your friends. You will have more helping hands and great ideas on board, and there's nothing wrong with having a little bit of fun on the side. Many great start-ups started with a team of **founders** rather than a single founder.

If it is not just you, but you and a group of friends who want to start a business together, then do the above as a group exercise. The group together will then have the skill of ideation, knowledge, access to prospective customers and the ability to get the money or seed **capital**—as it is called in the business world—to start your new business.

Write down your idea here and remember what it is. We're going to work and improve on this idea throughout the book.

#3
KNOW YOUR MARKET

What is a market? You would have probably learnt in your social sciences book that at the beginning of organized human civilization, people would gather in a central place in the village to exchange useful products. Even before the concept of money came into existence, they used a barter system—the exchange of goods and services. For example, I may have too many cows and you may have too many goats. So we may decide to exchange one cow for five goats. I may have too many apples and you may have too many strawberries, and we may exchange a dozen apples for a basketful of strawberries. But what happens when none of us wants strawberries?

That's where money came into the picture. In the above example, instead of strawberries, you could buy apples by paying for them in cash. If you think about it, strawberries would go bad in a couple of days if not eaten. Their value perishes. But that's not the case with coins and paper currency. I could keep the money I got by selling apples for two days or two years and it will still have value that I can use for buying anything I need. Money thus became a popular medium of exchange and store of value.

Money also helped expand markets. I could go to a faraway village with my money and buy bananas that my village did not have, instead of carrying with me strawberries that could perish before I even reach the market. Today, the concept of 'market' has evolved a great deal. We no longer need buyers and sellers to be present at the same time in the village square for buying and selling to happen. You can buy apples on BigBasket's website, pay for it via your preferred mode of payment and receive your order at your doorstep. Same with a pair of Nike shoes or a box of

Swiss chocolates. Markets have been becoming global for some years now.

For an entrepreneur just starting out, is the entire globe really your market? In theory, yes. But practically speaking, you are going to start with the market closest and most accessible to you and then think of the markets beyond those. So what is your immediate market? It's what comprises your probable customers: your family, neighbours, friends, cousins, schoolmates, teachers and anyone who may want to buy your product or service. Think of your market as not a 'shop' or a place but as a collection of your customers. And your first task as an entrepreneur is to get to know them and their needs better.

Let's say you are going to set up a lemonade business in the area you live in. Here are some simple ways to get to know your prospective customers and the market better:

a. What are the other places that sell lemonade in your area? List them out. What are the most interesting factors about them that you would like to note? They could include the price of a glass of lemonade, types of lemonade they sell, how they serve it, its temperature, their business hours and the type of customers that go there.

b. Now think of what you are going to do, your plan of action, the different flavours you'll sell, the adequate quantity to serve, how to serve, your working hours, the location of your business, how much you'll charge, etc. Think of all the details you'd like to know from your prospective customers.

c. Make a short survey form now. Make sure your questions are easily understandable and get you a definitive answer. The answers that you collect should help you make concrete decisions about your business. For example:

How do you like your lemonade?
- With ice
- Without ice

Which is your favourite lemonade flavour?
- Plain
- Mint
- Ginger
- Strawberry
- Spiced

d. Once your questions are ready, start collecting responses from your target customers. You can do a traditional paper form that your prospective customers could fill up, or you could interview them and fill it up yourself. You could also try going digital and make a survey form using tools such as Google, SurveyMonkey and Typeform, which you could send to people to fill up online. Either way, collect as many responses as you can.

e. Using simple analytical techniques that you must have learnt in school, figure out what your customers are saying. Do most of them like mint lemonade? Are most of them saying that Rs 50 for a glass is too steep? Are most of them excited about the idea of lemonade in a variety of flavours? Do they like it with or without ice? Make your decisions on the product, its packaging and pricing on the basis of the likes and dislikes of your customers. This gives you a good starting point, but remember to be fluid and approach everything with an open mind!

Make a survey questionnaire for your chosen product or service now:

....

....

....

....

....

....

....

....

....

....

....

....

....

....

#4
BEING DIFFERENT

Everybody knows how to make round wheels. But you want to be different and unique, so you decide to make square wheels. That's truly different, but is it useful or doable?

Think of uniqueness, differentiation and innovation from the customer's point of view. Does your customer actually need square wheels? If it is not solving their problems or fulfilling their needs, it is not useful and may not succeed.

Let's say when you collected information on all the other lemonade sellers in your area, you found out that there are five of them. All of them sell standard lemonade in a 200 ml glass for Rs 10–Rs 15 each. How are you going to be different? Why should someone want to buy lemonade from you and not from the other sellers? You can think of being different and innovative in many ways:

a. Product: Will your lemonade taste better? Are its ingredients better— maybe all organic? Your product must stand out and be the centre of attention.

b. Product range: Instead of offering the same old plain lemonade, will you have variants available? You need to think of the different variations your company will make and sell. But remember, less is more. Don't start with twenty different things—start small and perfect that.

c. Packaging: In addition to the 200 ml glass that every other seller in your area is offering, you could think of other options like presenting the lemonade in a takeaway glass, 1 L bottle and party pitchers. Interesting examples include brands like Paper Boat, which sells healthy drinks in a flexible pouch with a spout, and iD Fresh Food, which presents its vada batter in a squeeze-with-ease pouch. These are the brands that have invested heavily in getting their packaging right and have proved how convenient, useful and eco-friendly packaging is definitely advantageous.

d. Place: Think of the times when people crave a glass of lemonade the most. You can set up a stall inside a football stadium or a tennis stadium or even at the neighbourhood park where people go to jog or run. Notice how retail shops and fast-food joints are always well located for good footfall? You will realize that location plays an important role in attracting customers.

e. Price: When you have to choose between two similar products with different prices, will you choose the cheaper one? In most cases, yes. So, consider making your lemonade cheaper than your competitor's. Price is an important decision to make and we will talk more about it later in the book.

f. Branding: A catchy name and a catchy slogan can help a business like nothing else! If all other lemonade sellers are no-name stalls and if you create good branding around your stall, people will notice and recall your product better. Let's say you call your stall 'Funky Lemonade' and sell colourful lemonade in different flavours, you will be noticed among a crowd of other plain, no-variant, no-name sellers. Wondering what a 'brand' is and how you do 'branding'? Coming up in the next section, stay tuned!

g. Added benefit: You can distinguish your product on the basis of what else it provides. For example, it could be health benefits of drinking ginger lemonade. People love things that provide extra benefits in addition to the main value, especially when the extras are free. Like a temporary tattoo with your favourite chocolate milk! Everyone likes to get more value for the same price. Drawing attention to additional benefits that your product provides is a good way to differentiate it from the competition.

h. Environmental friendliness: You can be different and also socially responsible by serving only in reusable glasses or clay containers, for example. Disposable single-use plastic cups do enormous harm to our planet. Being conscious and being responsible can also bring you more customers who wish to support environment-friendly businesses.

How is your business going to be different and innovative? Write down all your ideas here:

....

....

....

....

....

....

....

....

....

....

....

....

....

....

START-UP STORY: WILDCRAFT
ENGINEERED FOR THE OUTDOORS

If you check with your parents and aunts and uncles who might have trekked and climbed mountains in the early '90s, you will hear stories of them trudging

through mud with wet canvas shoes, no tents and simple rucksacks that could not withstand the rains or the weight of the trekking gear.

Outdoor adventure gear from international brands was expensive and available only at a few places in India. The Indian brand that changed it all was Wildcraft.

A group of friends, passionate about the great outdoors, recognized the need for good-quality outdoor gear in India and then started Wildcraft in a garage in Bangalore sometime in the year 1998! Over the years, the team has stayed focused on design and production of gear that is durable, sturdy and resilient in the outdoor environment.

Today, the brand Wildcraft marks its presence in thousands of stores across hundreds of cities, has employed a few thousand people and makes a multi-crore **revenue**. It continues to innovate and make better products. If you connect their story with everything that we discussed in this chapter, what do you see? Does Wildcraft have a unique product—yes, outdoor gear! Do they have a well-defined market and customers—yes, people who like outdoor adventure activities! Can you find more such connects?

Wildcraft translated their idea into a successful growing company. What are some useful lessons from their journey that you would like to use while growing your idea?

Note them down here:

....

....

....

....

....

....

....

....

....

....

....

....

....

TWO

PRODUCT
WHAT AM
I SELLING?

Don't find customers for
your products, find products
for your customers.
—SETH GODIN,
AMERICAN ENTREPRENEUR,
WRITER AND SPEAKER ON
BUSINESS AND MANAGEMENT

#1
WHAT IS YOUR PRODUCT?

Let's say you want to start a cupcake-baking business from your home. What are the ingredients needed to make a cupcake? A basic cupcake recipe would ask for flour, butter, sugar, eggs, baking powder, chocolate chips and milk. So you get it all in place.

Now is this your product? No. What's next? Sift, beat, mix and bake the batter in the oven to make the cupcakes. Follow the instructions given in the recipe step by step.

Now is this your product? Somewhat. It is a little difficult to sell a cupcake that's sitting in a baking tray. What's the next step? You put it in a small paper box in which you can deliver the cupcakes.

Now is this your product? Almost there. What else can be done to enhance it? Instead of a generic paper box, you can make it into an appealing box with this catchline: 'Sweet Treats—A Boxful of Happiness!'

Now is this your product? Yes, it is!

When your customers order a box of cupcakes from you, they'll know that they need to ask for a box of 'Sweet Treats'.

Your product is not just a sum total of all its raw materials. The processes that go into making the product, its packaging and delivery, its name and associated qualities, all of it become a part of the product that the customer knows you for. Think of Lay's chips and you will end up thinking of not just one potato chip but the colourful packets of chips that you buy. Think of generic, no-name white canvas sports shoes and think of Nike, Adidas or Reebok shoes. All shoes have the same parts—the sole, the sides, the heel, the tip and the laces. What is different? Why are people loyal to one company over another? More importantly, how do you get your customers to favour you over all the other sellers?

#2
BRAND YOUR BUSINESS

Before we dive into this chapter, let's do a quick activity. Write down some examples of the following:

Social media apps

....

....

....

....

Stationery brands

....

....

....

....

PRODUCT—WHAT AM I SELLING?

Soft drinks

....
....
....
....

Soaps and shampoos

....
....
....
....

Football league teams

....
....
....
....

The names that you listed above are known as brands. Let's try to understand the concept of brands with a simple example. There are probably many small kirana stores and corner shops in your city that sell everyday items and sundries. You don't really care about where you buy your pencils and pen refills from, do you? But you care about the brand of the pen or the refill you use. Imagine if your favourite pen did not have a name! How can you find it on a store shelf among the hundreds of pens they sell? You will need to choose a specific pen by deciding upon a particular design, the ink and your writing style. Then knowing the brand name, which sells pens that match your preferences, makes it easy for you to ask for it specifically in a store. Clarity on all of these factors make it easier for the shopkeeper to immediately find the pen you want in his stock.

Brands create an assurance for customers about the quality and the product value they want. Brand names, graphic logos and catchy tag lines make a brand instantly recognizable and memorable. Think of McDonald's with its golden arches and Taco Bell

with its big bell **logo**. Think of Nike with its swoosh logo and the tag line 'Just Do It'. How do you achieve this for your product? How do you create a brand that makes a strong impression on your target audience? Here are some helpful pointers:

a. **Name:** What will your product or service be called? Think of an interesting name that conveys the qualities that are associated with your product or service. Do you think 'Strong Cupcakes' makes sense? Or do you think 'Sweet Moments' has a nice ring to it? Similarly, if you were starting a party planning business, would you prefer to name it 'Happy Party Planners' or 'Lullaby Party Planners'?

b. **Logo and colours:** It is not strictly necessary to have a logo with your brand name, but it does help in recognition. Again, think of what works well for your product. An image of a fluffy cupcake with a smile drawn on it will work very well for cupcakes but not as well if the product you're selling is potato chips! If you run a dog-walking service that's called 'Happy Puppy', an illustration of a cute puppy will make for a great logo. But the same illustration will be out of place if you provide a read-aloud service for senior citizens.

LOGO

NAME

TAG LINE

c. **Tag line:** Here is where you get to say something smart and memorable that people can immediately relate to. Keep it short, think of the emotions you want to evoke, qualities you want to highlight or a witty shout line for your brand. For example, for 'Sweet Moments' cupcakes, the tag line can be 'A Boxful of Happiness'. For the lemonade business, you could say 'Funky Lemonade—Fresh and Zesty!' A read-aloud service for senior citizens can be promoted with a tag line like 'We Read for You', which clearly articulates what your service is. The words 'sweet', 'happiness', 'fresh', etc., are what you want people to associate your brand with.

So what do you want your business to be known as? List out your ideas for brand names, logo designs and tag lines here. Get your creative juices flowing!

#3
DESIGNING A PRODUCT

While making decisions about your product or service, it is important to think about its design. Now don't think of design as decoration or art. As Steve Jobs said, 'Design is not just what it looks like and feels like. Design is how it works.'

Design thinking is at the heart of making products and services that are successful and provide a great experience to its users. You are designing your actual product as well as the branding for your product.

Let's think about the cupcakes business. What are the design considerations?

a. How big is the cupcake? Too small and people may find it pricey. Too big and people may find it difficult to hold and eat.
b. Is it possible to write a short message on top of each cupcake? Do people usually order your cupcakes to celebrate special occasions? Will people appreciate this customization?
c. Does it have any other decorations or icing on top?

d. How does the box accommodate the decoration on top? Does the cream stick to the box lid? If it does, you are likely to have disheartened customers.
e. Do you stick on the box a thank-you note for the customer?
f. What else does the box indicate? Are your contact details mentioned so that the customer can place the next order with ease? Where will it make most sense to print these?
g. Do you have to make the box look festive if your brand is catering to this mood? Will a ribbon or a bow do? Do you need to put anything else on it?
h. Are there seasonal or occasional decorations on the cupcake or the box?

I am sure you will be able to think of many other things that could help you design a better product that ensures better customer experience.

Design plays a role even in the way you conceptualize your production process. Big factories where cars are made are a good example of a well-designed production process, which makes sure that every car comes out looking exactly the way it is supposed to

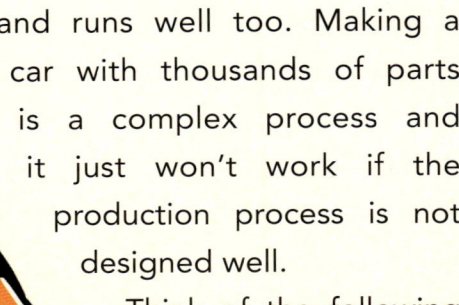

and runs well too. Making a car with thousands of parts is a complex process and it just won't work if the production process is not designed well.

Think of the following design considerations in the making of cupcakes:

a. What is the batch size of the cupcakes? How big is the oven? Too few at a time and you waste electricity, too many at a time and the cupcakes won't bake well.

b. If the order is for smaller or bigger numbers, how do you handle it? Or do you always bake a fixed number?

c. How do you optimize the use of all your baking tools and the oven to make sure there is no wastage of material or excessive clean-up needed?

d. After baking, where and how do you store the cupcakes? No customer wants stale cupcakes or flies on their frosting!

e. How do you design your entire baking process to ensure that you do it in the most efficient way—in the shortest time possible and in the most cost-effective manner?

When you consciously think about process design, efficiency and quality, you will realize that there are so many small ways to improve your way of working in a big way!

In case of services, think of the entire experience that you would like your customer to get. For example, let's say you are running a weekend reading club at a neighbourhood library for children. What are the little touches you could add to offer a delightful experience to your little customers?

a. Is the seating arrangement child-friendly?
b. Will you keep drinking water and a basket of snacks or treats for children?
c. Think of a welcome kit for new members—a bookmark, a small notebook to write book reviews, a reading list perhaps.
d. Will you have a noticeboard where you could put up recommendations and announcements about new books?

Customers remember a service for the experience it provides. Offer them a wholesome one and they will love you for it!

Write down some design decisions that you are going to implement for your product or service and then elaborate on how it would work. What would it add to your brand and customer experience?

....
....
....
....
....
....
....
....
....
....
....
....

#4
DESIGN THINKING

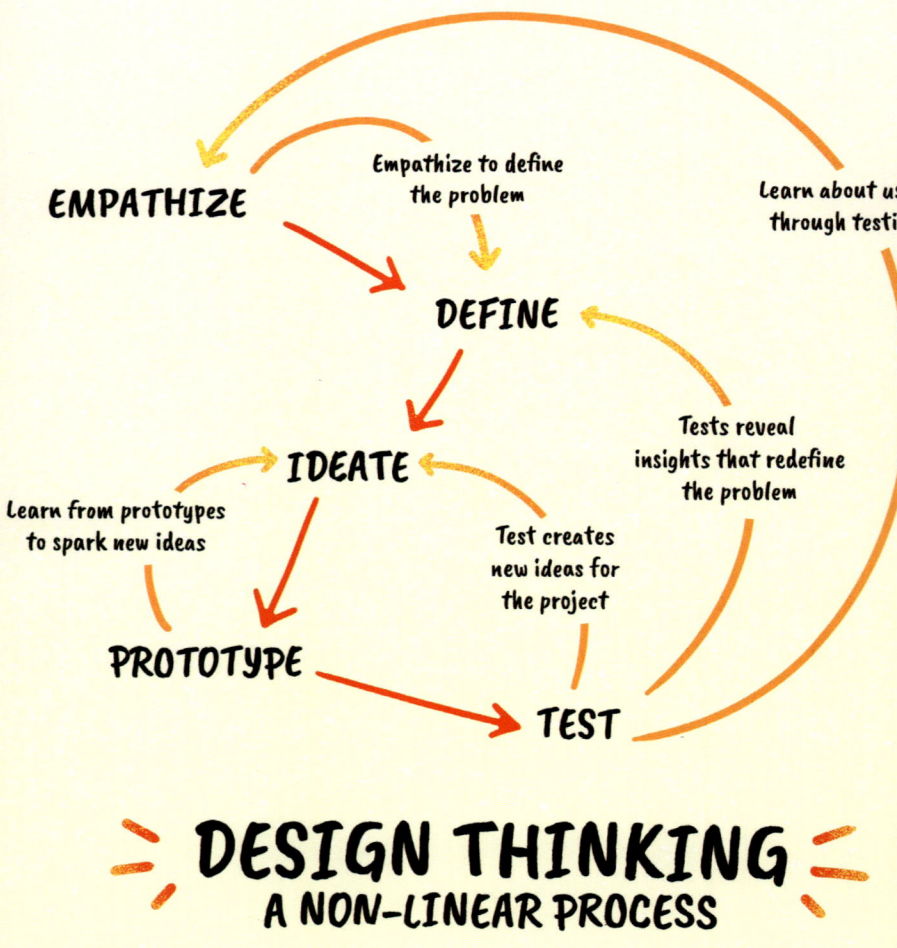

EMPATHIZE

Empathize to define
the problem

Learn about user
through testing

DEFINE

Tests reveal
insights that redefine
the problem

Learn from prototypes
to spark new ideas

IDEATE

Test creates
new ideas for
the project

PROTOTYPE

TEST

DESIGN THINKING
A NON-LINEAR PROCESS

Design thinking is a way of going about solving a problem, keeping in mind the user and their needs. When your starting point is 'the customers and their needs' rather than 'me and my product', you design a better product that actually addresses their needs. Otherwise there is a grave danger of designing a comb for bald people!

Empathizing with your customer means putting yourself in their shoes and trying to experience their ways of life. This works well as the bedrock of design thinking. That is what we were exploring when we were trying to know the market through surveys and customer interviews. Coming back to the example of a lemonade business, you will empathize with the prospective customers by understanding when they might feel thirsty and look for lemonade to quench their thirst. As I mentioned earlier, you have to be in the right place at the right time!

Understanding who your intended user is, where they can be found and what their precise needs are is an important next step. Being sensitive to the nuances and the tiny details is the key. For example, child-friendly seating arrangement is an essential factor when setting up a reading club meant for children, otherwise they might be uncomfortable and fidgety and not really enjoy the excellent storytelling that you may be doing.

Next on the list is: being aware of the possible alternatives and solutions. In how many different ways can you meet a particular need? If the customer is thirsty, lemonade is not the only solution—fruit juice, iced water or cold milk could also work. But if you decide to offer a sugar-free variant, you could end up gaining a niche audience that only looks for your brand. You have to know what particular need your product or service is going to address and how.

Now comes the most important part—the execution of the idea! At this stage, you make a prototype or a sample of your product. It will give you insights like nothing else can. For instance, you may find out that it is difficult to keep the milk chilled, but cold lemonade is easier to make and store with ice cubes.

We then move on to testing. Provide samples of your product to the customers. See how they like it. Collect their feedback. Ask them what they liked, what they didn't, what else they would like and so on. For example, do they prefer plain lemonade or flavoured lemonade? What kind of quantity are they looking for? Should the lemonade be served in a big glass or a small glass? Testing with users is the best way to know whether your idea and business will work.

Finally, it is showtime! You have designed and developed your product or service well. Do a prototype, get some customers and take their feedback.

Write down what you are going to ask the customers about your chosen product or service when you collect their feedback.

Your feedback matters

....
....
....
....
....
....
....
....
....
....
....
....
....
....
....
....

#5
START-UP STORY: iPHONE
REINVENTING THE PHONE

Steve Jobs, the co-founder of Apple who went on to become a legend, introduced in 2007 the first generation of smartphones called the iPhone, which revolutionized the way we look at touchscreens.

Phones had existed for decades before that, but as Jobs said in his famous keynote speech, they were neither smart enough nor easy to use. The iPhone became a trendsetter in many ways. It brought in the era of touchscreens, smart and user-friendly devices, mobile apps and much more. This smartphone was designed to fit in your palm and was made to be operated without a clunky keyboard and with a pointing device that you can't lose—your finger!

While the idea of making a phone wasn't new, Apple reimagined and made it differently. Apple became a company reputed for its product design and innovation. Many of its products like Macintosh, iPhone and iPod are loved by users for the excellent design thinking that has gone into making these products a joy to use. Apple was founded in 1976 and today it is counted among the most valuable companies globally.

Another great example of a user-friendly and neat interface is one of the most widely used messaging apps in the world—WhatsApp. Launched in 2009, it replaced the short message service, SMS, which gradually faded out as the go-to messaging service. In fact, you might want to check with your parents what the SMS-era was like! Built with a clean and intuitive design, WhatsApp works wonderfully well for new users as well without any training. It is used by billions of people around the world today. Its success can be measured by the fact that Facebook acquired it in 2014 for approximately $19 billion.

So, as a learning point from these trendsetters, what are the key elements you would like to keep in mind during the design thinking process?

THREE

MONEY
THE LIFEBLOOD
OF BUSINESS

Making money is art and
working is art and good
business is the best art.
—ANDY WARHOL,
AMERICAN ARTIST,
FILM DIRECTOR
AND PRODUCER

#1
MONEY MAKES THE WORLD GO ROUND

'The Man Who Saved Pumpelsdrop' is a popular short story by W.J. Turner. In this story, Pumpelsdrop is a small town going through a gloomy period in which businesses are not doing well. One day, a prosperous-looking man with an impressive title comes into town and places an order for two high-end luxury cars. The auto dealer is overjoyed with this new order and happily decides to buy jewellery as a Christmas gift for his wife. The jeweller is happy to receive a big order too and asks his wife to choose a gift for herself. The jeweller's wife in turn places an order for a fur coat. The coat maker is happy to receive this new order and also decides to spend some money. Thus starts a chain of everyone starting to spend all their savings. Soon enough, the town is bustling with busy markets and trade, and everyone is happy and carefree again. Just the hint of money and more business brings back prosperity into this little town!

Money truly is the lifeblood of any business. A business earns money, i.e., revenue through the sale

of its product or service but has to spend money, i.e., **expenses** to buy the raw material, labour and other services it needs for its day-to-day operations. When you start a business, you will encounter money matters too and hence it is important to understand how to manage your money wisely.

What are the channels through which money will come in and go out of your business?

....

....

....

....

....

....

....

....

....

....

....

....

....

....

....

Have you ever observed how your household runs like clockwork and how your parents handle money? Your parents are probably the earning members in the family who are bringing in salaries—this is their income. Things that they regularly need to pay for, like groceries, electricity, school fees and clothes, are their expenses. When your family earns more than it spends, it is able to save some money. But if the family spends more than it earns, it may have to take loans.

Businesses operate similarly. Money comes in as revenue or capital and is spent as expenses and investments. Broadly, businesses make profits when they earn more than they spend and they make losses when their expenses are more than their revenue. Let's dive into these concepts.

Capital is the money that you start your business with. In most cases, entrepreneurs start with some capital out of their own savings. As the business grows, it may need more capital to be infused for further growth. Other institutes or people often step in to invest money (capital investment), which may come in at several stages of a company's growth. If you follow business news, you would have read about start-ups, such as Ola, Swiggy and iD Fresh Food, receiving capital investments as they grew. These people and

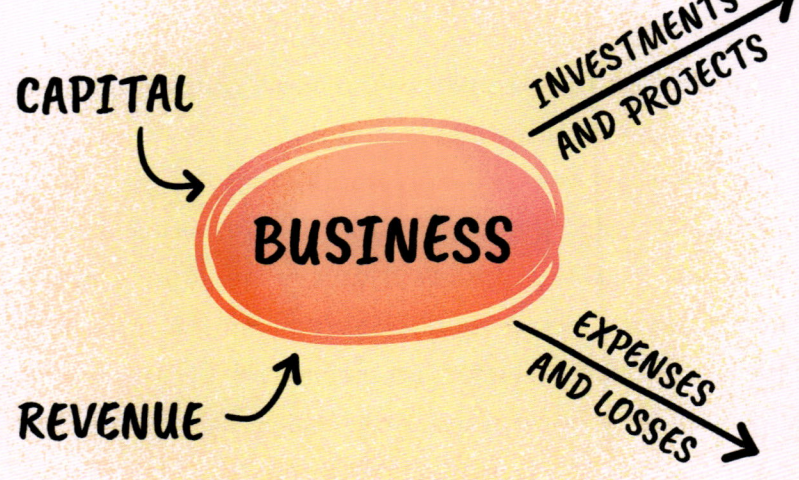

CAPITAL

BUSINESS

INVESTMENTS AND PROJECTS

REVENUE

EXPENSES AND LOSSES

institutions that provide such capital to businesses are known as investors. In turn they become part-owners or shareholders in the business.

Revenue is the money that your business earns through sales. It comes from customers who buy your product or service and is the income of your business. Making sales and earning revenue is the most crucial function in a business. If you do not make enough revenue, you will run out of money and your company may not survive. But if you make great revenue, you have a good chance of making handsome profits and building a good business. That's why you need to focus on keeping your customers happy and interested enough that they come back and buy more from you!

Expenditure is the money that a business pays for its expenses, like raw materials, salaries for the staff, office rent, advertising, etc. Expenses are a necessary part of running a business. You cannot make and sell lemonade without buying sugar, lemons and salt. What you need to watch out for is how you can keep the expenses under control while simultaneously increasing the business revenue. When your revenue exceeds the expenditure, you will earn profits.

Investments are a different kind of occasional spending that a growing business may choose to make to better their business in the long term. For example, if you run a thriving cupcake business that needs to churn out more products in a short period of time, you may need to buy one more oven for baking. That becomes an investment for long-term gain. However, buying material that you will need for day-to-day operations, such as flour, sugar and butter, is a form of expenditure and not an investment. Typically, investments are done over longer time periods and after careful deliberation, whereas expenses are a daily aspect of running a business.

#2
KEEPING TRACK OF EXPENSES AND REVENUE

No one likes to part with money. But unless you buy materials and services that your business needs, you can't produce anything to sell. As indicated earlier, there are some expenses that you will have to make to get your business up and running.

But what's important to know is how you can keep track of your money for your company. Here are some simple ways to keep things organized. Take a notebook and record every little thing that you pay for and procure for your business using this format:

DATE	EXPENSE DETAILS	AMOUNT (in Rs)
03-03-2020	SUGAR (1 KG)	50
04-03-2020	LEMONS (20)	100
04-03-2020	PAPER CUPS (50)	200
04-03-2020	POSTER PRINTING	50
	TOTAL	400

Now that we know how much we have spent, let's try to understand how much we have earned—the revenue. Every time a customer buys a glass of lemonade from you, the money that comes in is your revenue. You want to keep it growing, but for that it's important you keep track of how much revenue is coming in. Here is an example:

DATE	DETAILS	SELLING PRICE PER UNIT (in Rs)	TOTAL UNITS SOLD	AMOUNT RECEIVED (in Rs)
03-03-2020	PARK STALL	10	20	200
04-03-2020	FUNFAIR STALL	15	30	450
	TOTAL		50	650

Now try making your own table in your notebook. Think of the types of avenues you could explore for seeking revenue to grow your business idea.

#3
PROFIT OR LOSS?

You now know what you're spending on the purchase of your ingredients. But the job's not done! There's another interesting calculation for you to do and that is to calculate how much it costs to produce one unit of your product. This is a crucial step in deciding your **selling price**—the price you will sell each unit for—as well as planning for profitability. Profitability is the continuing ability of your business to consistently earn more money or revenue than the expenses incurred to turn a profit.

How do you calculate per unit cost? Let us take the costs of all the raw material that goes directly into the making of a glass of lemonade—all of these are your **direct costs**.

DATE	EXPENSE DETAILS	AMOUNT (in Rs)
03-03-2020	SUGAR (1 KG)	50
04-03-2020	LEMONS (20)	100
04-03-2020	PAPER CUPS (50)	200
	TOTAL	350

Total units produced: 50 glasses
Cost of one glass of lemonade:

$$\frac{\text{Total expenses}}{\text{Total units produced}} = \text{Rs } 7$$

Now you know that it costs you Rs 7 in direct costs to produce one glass of lemonade. Therefore, the minimum selling price will have to be more than Rs 7 per glass.

A business also incurs **indirect costs**. Sugar, lemons and paper cups were the direct materials that went into serving the product to a customer. These direct costs are also called variable costs because they go up or down depending on the quantity produced. More lemonade produced will mean more sugar, lemons and cups used. Now, what are the other activities that are crucial for running this business?

a. Your time and effort spent on making the lemonade
b. Your time and effort spent on selling and marketing the lemonade
c. Marketing and advertising costs that you incur for the printing of posters, their design, etc.
d. In some cases, you may have paid rent for setting up a stall.

All such indirect expenses are essential in the making of your product and need to be accounted for while calculating the profit of your business. Most times, indirect costs don't change with production quantity. Whether you make 100 glasses of lemonade or fifty, the cost of printing a poster or renting a stall will remain fixed.

DIRECT COSTS

INDIRECT COSTS

After taking all of these into consideration, your final profit and loss statement at the end of the year will look like this:

Profit and Loss Statement for the Year 2020

PARTICULARS	AMOUNT (in Rs)
TOTAL SALES OF LEMONADE (500 GLASSES)	60,000
TOTAL REVENUE (a)	60,000
DIRECT COST (500 GLASSES) (b)	35,000
OPERATING PROFIT (a – b)	25,000
INDIRECT COST FOR THE YEAR (c)	20,000
NET PROFIT (a – b – c)	5000

In your notebook, prepare your own profit and loss statement that summarizes your revenues, costs and expenses, made during each quarter and in the entire year, to understand how your business is doing.

Now, how do you think it works in the case of a business that provides services and not products? It is slightly difficult to understand the exact expenses and units sold in such set-ups. In most cases, there is not much material that is bought, but it is mostly skill-based work that you put in. Whether it is coding or design work or a library, it is your time spent in doing the work that will count the most. Let's say that your company designs websites for other companies. Think about how you can record the effort, the cost involved and the revenue for your business. The following format can be a good starting point:

Project: Website Design for Softy Cones—Cost Estimate

DATE	ACTIVITY	NUMBER OF HOURS	COST PER HOUR (in Rs)	TOTAL COST (in Rs)
03-03-2020	DESIGN WORK	4	500	2000
04-03-2020	CODING	6	500	3000
04-03-2020	TESTING AND FIXING	2	500	1000
04-03-2020	BUYING IMAGES FROM SHUTTERSTOCK			10,000
			TOTAL	16,000

In most of these businesses, there are two ways of calculating the price.

a. At the beginning of a project, you could make an estimate of the effort it would take for you to create something and provide a quotation to the client. After the client agrees to pay the price, you start the work. In such cases, you already know what your revenue from this project is. It is up to you to ensure that you complete the work within the estimated time and deliver. It is a good arrangement to have when the specifications or the scope of the projects are quite clear.

Your estimated cost for delivering the project covers the expenses you will incur and the time and effort you will spend. But as a business owner, you would also like to make some profit on each deal. So you can add a certain extra percentage to the cost—this is called a **markup**. You add the markup to the cost and the total is what you quote as your final price to the customer.

Say you add 20 per cent markup to Rs 16,000. This will mean another Rs 3200 get added to your costs and you can quote Rs 19,200 as the price for the project. In this case, your profit from this project will be Rs 3200.

b. You can charge the client a per-hour rate and keep working on the project as long as the client needs you to. This kind of arrangement is useful when the project specifications are not entirely clear in the beginning and hence both the parties do not know how much effort is needed. In such a case, you could quote an hourly rate, which is the money that you pay to your staff plus some markup, and charge your client for the number of hours you put in.

In the above case, you can quote an hourly rate of Rs 600 (base rate of Rs 500/hour plus 20 per cent markup). If the project takes 15 hours and you spend Rs 10,000 on the images for the website, your final invoice should amount to Rs 19,000 (600 x 15 = 9000, plus the cost of images). In this case, your profit from this project will be Rs 1500.

Here is a blank format that you can use to work out a sample quotation to provide for the projects you'll be carrying out in your service business:

....

....

....

....

....

....

....

....

....

....

....

....

....

....

....

....

#4
PRICING RIGHT AND BREAKING EVEN

As you would have realized in the previous examples, the price at which you sell your product or service is a key factor in determining your profit. If you charge a low price, you may not make enough revenue and profits. If you charge a price that's too high, you may not find enough buyers or clients. You need to strike the right balance between charging too low and charging too high. So what is the right price? It is difficult to give only one answer to this question, as pricing depends on many factors:

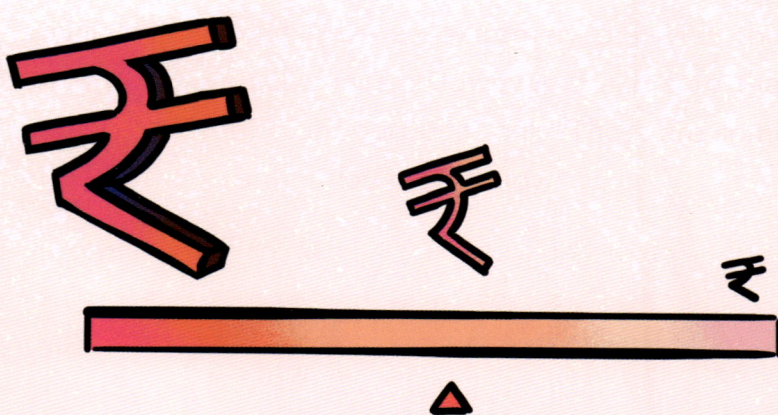

JUST RIGHT

a. **Costs and markups:** If you already know how much it costs to produce each unit of your product, you know the minimum level at which the price has to be set. The price cannot be below the cost per unit for too long, as that will land you in losses. Why would you set a lower price, you ask? This is explained a bit more in point c. In most cases, you can decide on the price with the formula 'cost + markup'.

b. **Effort estimation:** In case of service-based and project-based businesses, you may choose to quote the price based on the previously discussed formula of estimating effort on p. 74.

c. **Strategy:** If you want to capture a large market quickly, you may set a very low price. In extreme cases, you may even plan for losses in the beginning. Many new start-ups seek this route to get users hooked to their service. For example, most e-commerce businesses initially gave away freebies, like Swiggy did free home deliveries. This would mean higher expenses than revenue. Once customers get used to the convenience that their services offer, these businesses slowly increase the prices. Even a slight increase in prices and consequently **margins** makes a big difference to the overall profits of such start-ups because of the large customer base they have built through this strategy.

If your strategy is to become a premium brand, you may decide to keep your price point at a high enough level to be perceived as a brand that is of premium or superior value. For example, Mercedes-Benz cars are premium luxury possessions that people aspire to own. Their high pricing retains the aura that only a select group of people can afford to own one of these cars. These brands are not looking for a large number of customers, but their profit per customer is high.

What is the right pricing strategy for your business? Think about it.

Describe your pricing strategy here:

....

....

....

....

....

....

Now that you have understood the concepts of pricing, costing, revenue, expenditure and profits, another crucial concept to understand in business planning is the **break-even point**. This is a point at which your total revenue equals your total cost. Below this point, your business makes a loss and above this point, your business makes a profit. At the break-even point, your revenue is equal to cost thus giving neither profit nor loss.

Going back to the example of a lemonade business, this is how you will calculate the break-even point:

Direct variable cost per glass = Rs 7
(Cost of everything that goes
into the making of each glass)

Selling price per glass = Rs 12
(Price at which you sell
one glass of lemonade)

Operating profit
(per glass contribution
towards fixed cost, i.e., = Rs 5 (Rs 12 − Rs 7)
Selling price per unit − Direct
variable cost per unit)

Break-Even Analysis

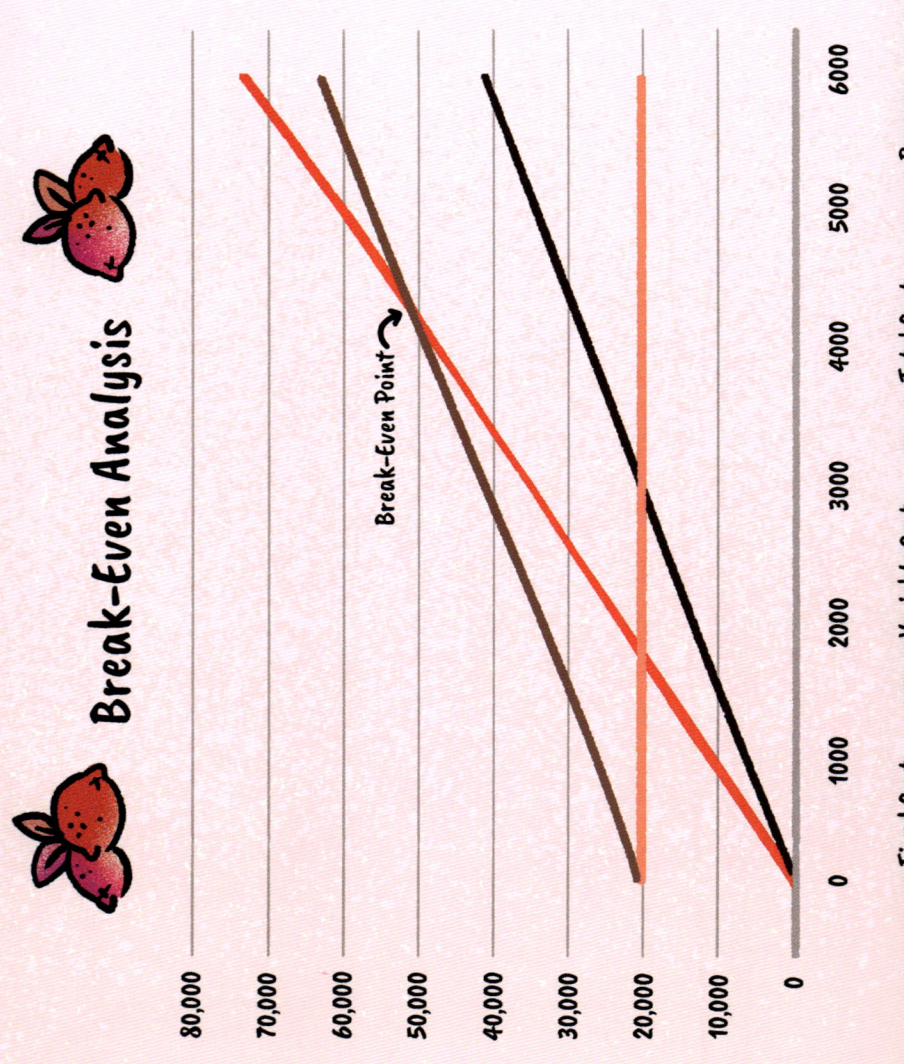

Break-Even Point

80,000
70,000
60,000
50,000
40,000
30,000
20,000
10,000
0

0   1000   2000   3000   4000   5000   6000

Fixed Cost   Variable Cost   Total Cost   Revenue

Total fixed cost to be covered   = Rs 20,000
(Costs that don't change much
according to the quantity produced)

Sales quantity (number of glasses)
needed to cover the fixed cost   = 4000 (Rs 20,000/
                              Rs 5)

Hence the break-even point for this business is at 4000 glasses. Let's cross-check this by making a profit and loss statement:

PARTICULARS	AMOUNT (in Rs)
TOTAL SALES OF LEMONADE (4000 GLASSES × Rs 12)	48,000
TOTAL REVENUE (a)	48,000
DIRECT COST (4000 GLASSES) (b)	28,000
OPERATING PROFIT (a − b)	20,000
INDIRECT COST FOR THE YEAR (c)	20,000
NET PROFIT (a − b − c)	0

At the break-even point of 4000 glasses sold, the costs are equal to revenue and there is neither profit nor loss. Every glass sold after this will give a profit of Rs 5.

Calculate the break-even point
for your business here:

#5
START-UP STORY: FLIPKART
INDIA'S BIG BILLION START-UP

Flipkart started as an online bookstore in 2007 out of a small two-bedroom apartment. As a business idea, it made perfect sense as books are best suited for selling online. It is not essential for the customer to touch, feel or try out the product before buying! Also, books are not fragile and are easy to ship considering the uniformity of shape and lightness. So, starting with the easiest category, Flipkart slowly moved on to selling appliances and electronics, then clothes and fashion items, and eventually became the place online to find anything and everything!

Today, it is one of the largest e-commerce businesses in India, selling items across many categories. It has been a trailblazer by being a risk-taker in a country dominated by small local shops everywhere. To establish trust in online shopping, Flipkart experimented with many innovations such as cash on delivery and building its own **logistics** and payment companies.

Flipkart's story of massive growth has been an inspiration for many entrepreneurs.

Globally, Amazon has been another e-commerce growth story. If you look at these businesses closely, you will realize the importance of building great distribution networks. You will also see the great advantage that capital can provide. Most e-commerce businesses attracted a large number of early customers by providing heavy discounts. Attractive prices got first-time online buyers to try it out.

Then the customers realized the convenience of shopping online and stuck to it. Amazon later added more innovations, such as Prime membership including free video streaming and music. All such tactics need companies to spend a lot in their early years and that's the advantage capital provides. Later as the business grows, companies start making profits that fuels further growth.

Where is the capital for your business coming from? How are you going to utilize it? How are you planning to build a distribution network for your business and grow it?

Note down your thoughts here:

....

....

....

....

....

....

....

....

....

....

....

....

....

....

....

....

....

 **FOUR**

PROMOTION
ARE YOU A WELL-KEPT SECRET?

You can't sell anything if you can't tell anything.
—BETH COMSTOCK,
AMERICAN BUSINESS EXECUTIVE
AND FORMER VICE CHAIR OF
GENERAL ELECTRIC

#1
HOW DO CUSTOMERS GET TO KNOW YOU?

Think of all the ad jingles you like. Think of all the brand tag lines that you like. Think of all the TV ads that you actually enjoy watching.

What is common among them? They appeal to you. You hum along to their tunes. You know the words too perhaps. You recall them. And that's the hallmark of good communication! It engages the recipient. It conveys its message well, and the message stays with the recipient. That is how the brand of your business gets built. Of course, great quality of your product or service is the first thing that customers will remember you for. But the next part they will recollect is the entire experience that they'll get during their interaction with you. And that is where your communication plays a role. Clear and effective communication helps both parties understand each other better. Good communication is important—not just in your marketing messages but also in how you describe your brand to the customer, how you make a sale happen and how you build a cordial relationship with your regular customers.

A hit new single by your favourite band, the next Marvel movie, a discount on the best new phone in the market—how do you get to know about them? Maybe sometimes on TV, sometimes through news, online ads, reviews on the internet, a TikTok video, SMS, newspaper pamphlets or even your friend's recommendations—right? All of these are ways through which the producers or creators of the products and services let you know about their new offerings, benefits, new features, discounts and special schemes. Promotion is an important tool of communication that connects the producers with the consumers.

Before you start thinking about your promotional strategies, let's see the channels that you can use to get in touch with your customers. First, you need to identify who your customers are. Look around you. Your parents are probably newspaper readers, but your older siblings might be reading news online. The magazines and the social media pages that you follow and what your sibling follows might be different from your interests. A sports product might appear on the Sportskeeda website, but a fashion product ad would get better attention on Instagram as the kinds of users are different on each platform. People who follow *Bhoole Bisre Geet* on Facebook and people who watch the latest Marshmello videos on YouTube are decidedly different from each other. You need to know who your target audience is, what they typically do, where you can find them and the best way and time to reach them for your promotional communication to be effective.

ONLINE

OFFLINE

Hi!

95

Broadly, you can think of different communication channels as:

a. **Online:** Website, social media, emails, listing sites
b. **Offline:** In-person pitch, pamphlets and brochures, phone calls, SMS, mobile ads

Of course, large businesses use many other channels such as outdoor billboards and hoardings, TV and radio advertising, celebrity endorsements and more. But typically, these are much more expensive. As an entrepreneur with their own small business, you can start with an affordable mix of online and offline channels effectively.

#2
BEING SOCIAL ONLINE

Website

Your company's website is an online platform to showcase your brand and for people to know more about your business, products or services, prices, working hours and how to reach out to you. You can feature  testimonials and reviews from satisfied customers, you can announce new product launches—it's really up to you how you make the most of your website.

Typically, these are the website types one has to choose from:

a. **Static content website:** This website is meant to provide information about your business, but no actual business happens on the site. Most offline businesses will have this type of website design. For example, a lemonade business can have a static website that mainly provides information about the products, flavours and where it is located.

b. **E-commerce website:** This website *is* your business, which means that your actual business happens on the site. Your products and services are listed and showcased on this site. People can place an order for whatever they like and then pay for it online. If it is a digital product (e.g., a Kindle e-book), you can deliver it to them by doing an online transfer. If it is a physical product (e.g., cupcakes), you will need to send it to them through a courier or delivery service.

c. **Application:** A web or a mobile app is a product in itself, for example, a simple online game. In such cases, your website is much more complex with many functionalities and will require extensive technical knowledge to build. Your customers can pay for the app usage via subscription or a one-time purchase.

In either case, a website is one of the most important online spaces for your business. It's like having a home address in the online world to let people know where to find you. When people search for a particular product or service on Google by typing 'best cupcakes nearby', you would want your website to show up in the search results. That is how people will discover your business and buy from you.

Making a content website is not a very difficult or expensive task. If you are well versed with web development, you can design and code your own website. But even if you're not, you can use one of the many free website-creation tools available these days that help you build a site in a few hours, such as Google Sites, Wix or Weebly. Other options include creating a WordPress site, which is simple and comes with many ready-made templates yet gives you much room for customization and creativity.

If you are building a website for selling your products, you can consider using simple e-commerce site platforms, such as WooCommerce or Shopify. These let you set up a product catalogue to be able to showcase your offerings easily. For accepting online payments, you will need to integrate an online payment gateway on your site. There are fairly simple options, such as Instamojo, Razorpay and PayTM, which you can look up. You can direct your payment receipts to a linked bank account.

For web or mobile applications, you need to consider an extensive technical backend. It helps if you are a coder or have good coders and technically qualified people on your team.

At this stage, you might need to get guidance from an expert on carrying out the website and payments set-up safely. It's always a good idea to be aware of cyber safety and data privacy—for yourself and for your business!

Before you start making your website, it is best to have a clear idea of what it should look like and how it should work. You'll need to make a simple skeleton—called a wireframe—of your website. This is an extremely important step as this is the part where you'll be able to spot any errors or potential flaws in the design. In the wireframe, you will need to create placeholders for images, text content, clickable buttons, etc. Once you have the wireframe ready, it will be easy to design and develop the site using any of the page-creation tools.

So, if you have a cupcake business and want to set up an e-commerce website for it, here's what the wireframe should look like:

Use the space below to draw a wireframe for the business idea that you have in mind:

Social Media

Social media has completely revolutionized the world of marketing. Social media lets a business talk to their customer directly, wherever the customer may be! Just look at the average number of social media apps you and your friends frequently use. TikTok, Facebook, Instagram, Twitter, Snapchat, WhatsApp, SHAREit, ShareChat and whatnot! For professional networking, there is LinkedIn, for video content, you have YouTube. For pictures alone, there is Pinterest. All of these have the potential to build the brand of your business and actually help you do more business, if used right.

Why should you take social media marketing seriously?

a. Social media allows you to connect with your target customer directly and drive the message home.
b. It is quick and easy.
c. It is almost free.
d. Social media makes it easier for new customers to discover your business.
e. You can create and control your brand image and messaging the way you want.

How can you crack the social media success code? Here are some quick tips:

 a. On most social media platforms, personal handles or pages and business handles or pages are different. For example, personal handles on Facebook and LinkedIn have a limit on how many friends or followers you can have, but business pages don't. So make sure that you open an account for your business by choosing the right category.

 b. Only text content does not attract as much attention as posts with visual elements, such as pictures or videos. Each platform has its own specifications, such as character or word limit for the post too. Be aware of those and draft your posts accordingly.

 c. All social media platforms provide detailed insights for business pages. You will be able to see the reach, engagement, clicks, followers and

other performance parameters for the posts and the page. These parameters will tell you how many people saw your post, liked or shared it; how many clicked on it to find out more; and how many commented on it. It also tells you where your customer is located, at what time they're most active, what kind of content they prefer and much more! Review these insights and analytics carefully to understand what works for your audience.

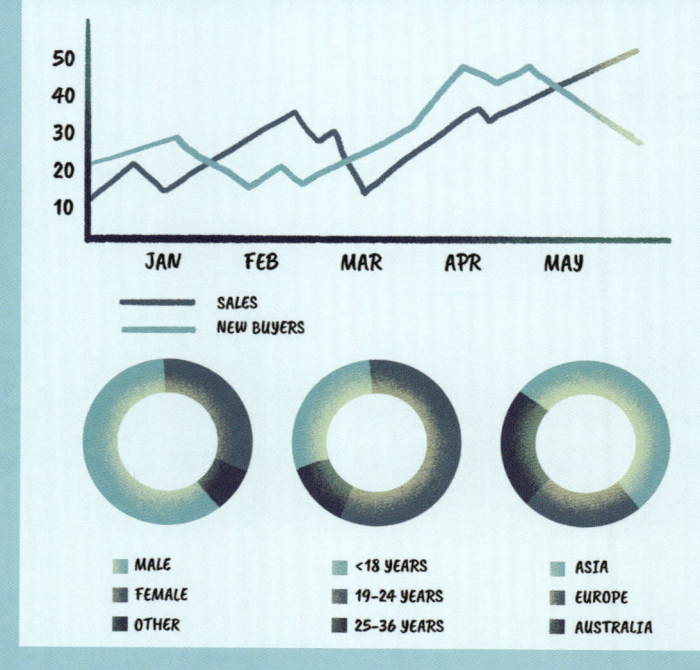

d. On most social media platforms, you can also do paid publicity. It ensures that your content reaches the target audience in a streamlined manner. While paying, you can define what kind of audience you want by selecting their city, age group, gender and other factors. Typically, these are flexible budgets and payments. So you can invest a small amount to learn how paid social media marketing works. But do remember to remain within the sensible marketing budgets that your business can afford, and do not go overboard with paid marketing. Critically assess the results that you get before deciding to spend more.

e. Be aware of the dangers of being too dependent on social media. Don't you feel good when you see the number of likes on your Instagram post going up? And don't you feel a little disappointed when no one likes or responds to your post? It is natural for you to react like that, but those reaction patterns are the problems that you need to be aware of and stay away from. Research shows that these platforms have an ability to provide instant gratification to the user, which leads to the user becoming too dependent on them, but unfortunately, this doesn't necessarily convert into sales.

So, the bottom line is: use social media as a business marketing tool but within limits, and know that it is not the only thing that needs to work for your business!

What would you like to tell your customers about your business? How would you introduce your products and your brand to prospective customers? Write down a few sample posts that you think will work well to promote your business on social media:

....

....

....

....

....

....

....

....

....

....

....

....

Emails

Email is another excellent form of non-intrusive personal communication with your target audience. Your email lands in the personal mailbox of the recipient and gets the attention that you want.

How will you get the email addresses of your customers? These are some of the ways to do so:

a. Ask for the email ID at the time of user registrations.
b. Create a quick feedback form that your customers will have to fill up with information, including the email ID.
c. While designing your website, make a form where people can register to receive updates about your business via email.

Email marketing can be an extremely powerful tool for growing your business. However, make sure that you use it for the right purposes only. There are some ethical practices that you must follow:

a. Do not share your email database with anyone. People trust you with their email addresses—respect that trust and use the email address for genuine communication only.

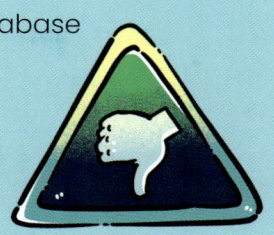

b. If people ask to be unsubscribed from your list, do so. Do not continue to send them mails.

c. Do not spam. Send only relevant and useful emails. Bombarding your customers with too many messages or unprofessional mails will drive them away.

Once you have a long list of email addresses of your customers, you will realize that manually sending mails to each one of them becomes a tedious and time-consuming job. At this stage, you can consider using a mass-mailing service, such as Mailchimp or Constant Contact—there are many out there. These services help you to store all the email addresses in an efficient and organized manner and design eye-catching emails with colours, pictures and clickable buttons.

You also get the choice of creating custom lists of certain customers when sending out specific messages.

Make sure that you draft the content well and convey the message effectively. What are some of the points that you need to pay special attention to?

a. An effective subject line: Most of us glance at a subject line of a new mail in the inbox and then make a decision about opening it. If the subject line says something meaningful and relatable for the recipient, there is a greater chance that your email will be opened and read. Here are some examples of catchy subject lines:

'Zesty new flavours and offers at Funky Lemonade'
'Have you tried our new Hulk Lemonade yet?'
'Guess which new flavours are popular at Funky Lemonade this season?'

b. Crisp and clear message: Short emails, which can be quickly read and understood, do better. Use reader-friendly fonts, colours and design. Make sure there are no spelling and grammatical errors. Shorter and direct sentences work well. Make sure that all the important points in your message stand out.

c. Call to action: If you want the recipient to take an action immediately after reading your mail, make it easy for them to do so. For example, if you end  your mail with 'Visit us now', add a map link right after that. If you say 'Call us', do mention your phone number.

What will your promotional email to your customers say? Draft one here:

Listing Sites

When your target customers search for the product or service you offer online, will your business show up in the search results? That is a key test for any business today. You want to be visible to your customers. Because, unless they know you exist and where to find you, how will they find you?

There are some steps you can take to make your business online search-friendly.

a. Tag your location in Google Maps with the correct name, description and address.

b. Make sure your website uses all the keywords that people may search for. What will people search for if they want to order cupcakes? Maybe 'cake order', maybe 'cupcakes', maybe even 'birthday cake'. Think about these possibilities while writing the website content. When people type in a search term, search engines, such as Google and DuckDuckGo, use that term to find relevant websites. If those words are found on your website pages, your site will show up in the search results and that's how your prospective customers are going to find you! You'll need to constantly keep updating the keywords you're using. It's tedious but an essential step to being 'found' on the vast internet!

c. Register with online directories, such as Justdial, IndiaMART and Zomato, based on what your business is and where your customer might look for you. Keep an eye out for local pages and online groups in your area.

#3
BEING PRESENT OFFLINE

Offline channels are sometimes costlier than online channels. But then face-to-face communication with the target customer is also more powerful. It helps in building credibility and trust with your customers. We all like to interact with known people and faces rather than strangers, don't we? Offline outreach helps you build that connect with people. What are some of the easy, quick and efficient ways to do it?

a. Phone calls: For sourcing phone numbers, you can use the same techniques and follow the same set of ethical guidelines that were pointed out for email addresses. If you decide to do telemarketing, make sure that you call at the right time and are not intrusive. After seeking permission for a quick conversation, talk about your offering and see if the listener is interested. Have a well-written and rehearsed speech ready, but more importantly, LISTEN! It is important to understand your listener's point of view rather than convincing them of your own. Before completing the call, make sure you're able to get an idea of the listener's level of interest, which will ultimately lead to one of these things—don't call them again, or send them more information or that they're interested in buying from you!

b. SMS or WhatsApp messages: Again, the same rules about privacy and ethics apply here. Do not spam people. Use your communication to inform and persuade but within the limits of pleasant and civil conversation.

c. Posters: Posters displayed at the right places can be effective promotional tools. For example, is there a noticeboard at the neighbourhood park, on which you can put up a poster that lets people know that your lemonade stand can be visited at the gate every evening? Well-designed posters are sure to attract attention. Don't forget to include your contact information and a call to action, such as 'Order now' or 'Visit us'. You can make posters online for free, using tools that provide ready-made templates and a wide variety of design options.

d. Pamphlets: Pamphlets can be delivered from door to door or distributed at places with high footfall, such as parks, malls, markets, etc. Pamphlets are good for mass publicity in a certain area. Again, you can try out online tools to quickly design your own pamphlet for free. The key is to make it visually appealing and full of useful information so as to gently nudge readers to interact with your business.

Think of the posters and pamphlets that you have liked. What was good about them? Think of the ones that you really disliked. What were their flaws? Learn from their mistakes and design your own perfect poster or pamphlet:

#4
COMMUNICATING AND CONNECTING

Good communication is an art to be practised. But along with all the creative aspects, a little bit of science by way of frequency of communication and following a consistent format helps. Your goal is to build a good relationship with your customers. They should trust your brand, be able to recall it quickly and stay loyal to your brand. A happy and loyal customer is a great asset for any business. How do you use your communication campaigns effectively to achieve this?

For starters, figure out the right frequency of communication. You don't want to be a nuisance by sending too many messages, but you don't want to be forgotten either! So just the right message at the right time is what you need to deliver. Find out what works for your customers by observing customer behaviour, having conversations with them and keeping track of sales data. Once you find an effective formula, repeat and keep checking periodically what needs to change. Non-intrusive mass communication formats are easier but impersonal. Personalized communication directly delivered over the phone or in the mailbox of the customer has a greater chance of being noticed but is also intrusive. Striking the right balance is the key to success.

Let's say you want to send a thank-you note to your regular customers because you recently got your thousandth order. How do you say it with a flourish? Let's design an email here:

#5
START-UP STORY: BOOKMYSHOW
NOW SHOWING . . .

Imagine eagerly waiting for the final movie in your favourite series. Let's say you had your heart set on watching it on day one of its release. So you go to the movie theatre and join a kilometre-long queue. After an hour-long crawl to the ticket counter, you are told that the tickets are sold out! And the same story repeats the next day and the next weekend because you don't have time to book the tickets in advance during the week.

This is how people used to buy movie tickets before the year 1999. What made the process easy so people could book from anywhere, anytime? BookMyShow! Started by three friends in 1999, BookMyShow is presently the largest entertainment ticketing service, selling not just movie tickets but also tickets for concerts, events and sports.

The journey was not always smooth for these entrepreneurs, but they stuck to it. Today, search for 'latest movies' and see what shows up first!

How did BookMyShow create such a market for itself? Eye-catching graphics, blog posts across categories, an active social media presence and focused mobile marketing are some of the things they did well. Look for the clues on their website and social media, keep an eye out for movie promotions, look for their freebies with certain banks and cards and observe the messages and offers that their existing customers receive. Truly a lesson in good marketing!

Think of all other examples of impressive marketing and branding that you see all around you. Amul posters showcasing the brand's trademark humour with the Amul girl, Maggi with its 2-Minute pitch, Flipkart with kids in their ads, PayTM with its catchy jingle—what else comes to your mind?

What kind of marketing plan do you wish to execute for your business? Good logos and some catchy lines? Can you form some useful partnerships with other brands? Can you think of some exciting offers for your customers? Note them down here:

....

....

....

....

....

....

....

....

....

....

....

....

....

 **FIVE**

GROWTH STAGE
BEING A BUSY BUSINESS

It always seems impossible until it is done.
—NELSON MANDELA, SOUTH AFRICAN POLITICAL LEADER AND PHILANTHROPIST

#1
DO YOU HAVE A BUSINESS?

You are operating a business only when people are buying from you. Making a great product, setting up social media, putting up nice posters is when you're putting the pieces together, but a business is truly born when sales happen. The question is how do you make sales happen?

a. Attention to customer needs:
Customers do not always describe their needs well, so you may need to read between the lines and understand what exactly the need is. The customer may say, 'I feel very thirsty during my run in the park.' Will this customer buy a glass of lemonade before entering the park or is he looking for a bottle of lemonade that he can carry with him during the run? Listening carefully and observing customer behaviour are the best tools for understanding your customer.

b. Relevant value proposition:
A popular saying goes: 'Are you selling a comb to a bald man?' Make sure your product or service is relevant to the customer you have in mind. A glass of cold lemonade would be a good product to sell to runners, but a box of chocolate desserts, not so much.

c. Where is your customer?: Time and place play a huge role in how well your product sells. A fancy accessories stall will do well in a mall with high footfall, but will it do well if set up in a quiet, suburban residential neighbourhood, away from the main road? A cotton candy seller may do well at a funfair or if he sets up his stand outside a school after closing time. But will he sell anything outside a school from 6 a.m. to 8 a.m.? Know where and when to find your customers to make effective sales.

d. The sales pitch: How you describe your product and its benefits, how you handle questions from your customers, how well you build a rapport with the customer translates to how well your product will sell. Have you ever observed how vegetable and fruit hawkers sell? 'Fresh green spinach, such tender leaves—you must buy it!' 'Best red strawberries, fresh from Mahabaleshwar, season is ending soon, take two boxes!' They even remember what your mother buys, what you like to eat and what kind of mangoes your family will buy. Understand what makes an instant impression on customers, what they specifically like about your products and build your sales pitch with it.

e. Reduce friction: Make it easy for your customer to buy from you. Think of what information they may need before they make a decision to buy and provide it proactively to customers. Make it easy for them to place an order and make a payment. For example, will you accept an online order or an order via a text message? Will you accept payment digitally via PayTM or UPI so that the customer is not scrambling to find cash? A frictionless, smooth process will reduce the dropout rate that occurs at every step in the entire selling process.

f. Win-win is the way: A business does well when both the seller and the buyer win. When customers buy something from you, they are parting with money. Let's say a woman buys a glass of lemonade for Rs 20 from you, drinks it, feels refreshed and is happy. She thinks that her money was well spent. There is a good chance that she will buy from you again and even order a large pitcher for her next party as she found great value in your product.

On the other hand, you are trying to make revenue. You earned Rs 20, you felt happy. You won too! You would want to keep the business going. This is a win-win situation for all! But imagine if the customer thinks the lemonade serving is insufficient and Rs 20 is too much to pay for it. She feels unhappy and decides not to buy again from you. Then it's a loss for both of you.

In another scenario, imagine if she bargains and you sell a glass of lemonade for Rs 10—half the price. Then you feel unhappy because you did not make the desired amount of money that day. You might lose the motivation to put in effort. That's a loss again for all.

In a good business transaction, both parties win. Both derive enough value and motivation from the transaction to want more. And that's what keeps the business going!

No business ever gets built without an effective sales pitch. What's yours? Write it down here:

....
....
....
....
....

#2
GROWING AND ORGANIZING YOUR BUSINESS

So you started a business, got some customers and made some revenue. Congratulations! But how does a small business grow from its first stage?

The entrepreneurs who start the business are also called founders. Some businesses are started by a solo founder, some by a team of co-founders. Founders are usually the first owners of the business.

As was pointed out earlier, one important ingredient that goes into the making of a business is the capital. You may have borrowed the capital from your family and friends with a promise to return it. This type of capital is called **debt**. Sometimes, you may find an investor who wants to give you money and become a part-owner of the business. This type of capital is called equity investment.

Most big start-ups that you are familiar with—Facebook, Oyo, Swiggy, BookMyShow—have all raised crores of rupees in capital. Capital is the fuel that powers the journey of a new small business, helping it grow big.

As a small business grows, a single founder or even a team of founders will not be enough to manage it after some time. You will need to hire people and build a team to run the business. Slowly, functional teams start forming. In any business, you will typically see the following functions and teams:

a. Production or Delivery: In a product business, this team looks after the production or manufacturing of the goods you are selling. So, for example, their responsibilities would include the making and bottling of lemonade. In service businesses, this team manages the delivery of the service to the customers. An example of this would be someone assigned for design and coding of a website for your website development business.

b. Procurement: This team buys the material needed for the business. They find the best vendors to buy from, how much to buy and when, where to store the material and how to keep it safe. This could be the lemons, sugar or even the quality labels for the bottles.

c. Marketing and Sales: This team is in charge of promoting your business, getting more and more people interested in buying from you and managing the sales. They are the people who bring in the revenue for the business—directly, if you're the sales team, or indirectly, as is the case with marketing.

d. People or Human Resources: When you think of your school, is it just the building and the benches and the ground that come to your mind? You also think of your teachers, your friends, the fun you have during recess—don't you? Similarly, an organization, a business is built by people. A business needs people to keep it running. This team ensures that the right people join your company, their well-being is taken care of and that they grow the business along with the founders.

e. Finance: As I said earlier, money is the lifeblood of any business. The finance team makes sure that money is being managed well, that you do not spend more than you earn and that you make profits! They would be able to let you know if you've overshot your marketing budget and how to increase your profits in a smart way.

f. Administration: A business needs support on many fronts—administrative, such as managing paperwork; legal support to know more about government permissions and the filing of tax returns; and IT and tech support to keep computers and networks running without glitches. No one wants to work with a website development company that has servers that keep crashing!

Running a business is like participating in a team sport. Each member of the team is valuable but none more valuable than the team itself. The team needs to work together to win. Similarly, in a business, each team member needs to play their functional role well for the business to succeed. That's where leaders become important. Can you imagine a cricket or football team without a captain? It would be a bit chaotic, don't you think? In a business organization too, you will see a captain, i.e., the chief executive officer (CEO) and a vice-captain or the president. A business leader manages the team, keeps it motivated and solves its issues to make sure that they deliver well and win.

As a business grows and starts hiring people and forming teams, it will need to be moulded into one of the following mentioned forms of business organizations:

a. Sole proprietorship: In this form of business, it is the sole founder who owns the business. He or she is in charge of running the business and receives the profits or losses as the case may be.

b. Partnership: Several co-founders come together and form a partnership to start and run a business. They jointly run the business and share the profits or losses.

c. Company: A company is a separate legal entity. It is an artificial person created by law that makes profits or losses. It can receive capital from many people—founders as well as other investors who may invest money but not take part in running the business. Most big businesses are companies with a large amount of capital and they employ a number of people to run the business. There are different types of companies: one-person company, private company, public company, etc. A company can decide how much of its profit will be shared among its owners and investors.

Many a time, businesses adopt different forms as they evolve. They start as a small business run by a few people, grow into a company employing many more people, become bigger and then turn into companies that operate across the world, have offices in every country and are counted as industry-leading organizations. Do you know that a company as big as Amazon was started by a solo founder—Jeff Bezos? Many of the popular tech start-ups, such as Facebook, Microsoft and Google, were started by college students!

List out some of the big businesses you know. Find out what form of organization they are. Do read about their history to know how their form changed—it'll be super interesting.

....

....

....

....

....

....

....

....

#3
SOCIALLY RESPONSIBLE AND SUSTAINABLE BUSINESS

A business is not an island by itself. It is intricately linked with the society. You as the business founder, your teammates, your customers, your suppliers—everyone is a part of the society. And we all live on this beautiful planet—the only planet that supports human life. A business cannot work in isolation and function only to make profits without considering the people and Planet Earth. A business uses resources, such as water, raw material, electricity, most of which have an environmental cost. Sometimes production processes

result in pollution and waste material. These need to be taken care of to ensure no harm is caused to the people around us or the environment. A business, which ignores these considerations and focuses only on its own profits, is an irresponsible business and cannot survive for too long. While there are some big corporations that have not been very mindful of the environment in the past and have been responsible for causing environmental damage, there is greater awareness and movement among people pushing such companies to change their practices today. As a business owner, keep these three Ps in mind: Planet, People and Profits.

For example, the lemonade that you serve to customers will be consumed in a few minutes and will lead to satisfaction, but what if it was served in a disposable plastic cup? That cup—in a garbage can first and in a landfill later—will live on for a few hundred years polluting the environment! Is a moment's convenience worth centuries of agony? Certainly not. So, be conscious and be eco-friendly in your business decisions. Everything you do, every step you take, every decision you make will have an environmental impact. Here are some ways to build an eco-friendly business:

a. Do not use any single-use plastics.

b. Do not waste any material.

c. Know how to manage the garbage. Segregate and dispose it off properly.

d. Keep your business surroundings clean.

e. Avoid the use of chemicals. If you are in the food business, buy local, seasonal and naturally grown produce.

f. Optimize the use of paper.

g. Avoid polluting the natural resources, such as air, water and soil. If your business produces any toxic material, it is important to dispose it off safely without causing harm to the environment and people around you.

Depending on the type of business you are doing, you will have different opportunities to take care of the environment and society. Big companies in India have a legal obligation to spend a part of their

profits on creating positive social impact through corporate social responsibility (CSR) activities. Small businesses can always choose to be aware and active on this front too.

In addition to being kind to the planet, being kind to people is equally important. Make sure that the working conditions at your place of business are healthy and pleasant. Happy employees build happy and successful businesses. Being fair and kind to people around you is of utmost importance. One of the challenges for an organization lies in building a culture of diversity and inclusion. But what do these terms actually mean? It means that other people may be very different from you when it comes to language, background, education, personal opinions and way

of working. That is diversity. What a business needs to practise is inclusion. Recognize that there could be multiple ways of doing something right. Make room for diversity. Include different people in your discussions and decision-making. It's like making new friends—everyone may not like the same movie and the same flavour of ice cream, but the fun lies in hanging out with a new friend!

What are some planet- and people-friendly steps you would like to take to build a healthy and successful business?
Let's make a list here:

....

....

....

....

....

....

....

#4
IT TAKES A VILLAGE!

So how has it been so far? Being an entrepreneur and building your own business is a thrilling journey, isn't it? You are in it to create value, feel good about what you are doing and make your customers happy.

This journey can potentially transform you as a person. You learn to become resilient and humble. It gives you confidence that you can achieve anything. It gives you the joy of creation and accomplishment. Nothing is more fulfilling than that!

But this journey is also like a rollercoaster ride. Along with its highs come the lows, similar to when you have a sick feeling in the pit of your stomach on a roller coaster and you feel afraid. Sometimes you do not know how to do something. Sometimes you are confused and don't know which way is better. And there are no textbooks to give you the right answer. Every business and its founder are a unique combination. The way they solve problems and succeed is unique too. No one has any ready-made answers. Many entrepreneurs did not succeed in their first venture. Many went through multiple ideas and multiple ventures before becoming successful. Ventures may fail, but entrepreneurs don't. They learn from each thing that did not work and do better next time. It is an exciting yet uncertain journey.

So how do you deal with so much uncertainty? Fortunately, there is help available. Many entrepreneurs benefit a great deal by talking to their advisers and mentors. Typically, these are experienced people who have been part of many businesses and have seen the problems they faced and the solutions they came up with. They can offer guidance based on their experience. Think of them as team coaches!

Where do you find them though? Some may be around you as part of your family and network of friends. Some are available through more formal and organized institutions that support young entrepreneurs. Many academic and other institutions today run Entrepreneurship Development Programmes (EDP), **start-up incubators and accelerators**—all meant to provide support to budding entrepreneurs. These programmes offer coaching on business skills, sometimes workspace and some seed capital to start with. The most valuable help that all of them offer is connecting with mentors and prospective customers.

Here are some helpful links of resource centres in India that foster entrepreneurship:

a. TiE Young Entrepreneurs (TYE)
    https://bangalore.tie.org/programs/tye/
b. National Entrepreneurship Network (NEN)
    http://staging.nen.org/
c. Entrepreneurship Development Institute of India (EDII)
    https://www.ediindia.org/

d. Atal Innovation Mission (AIM)
   https://niti.gov.in/aim
e. Startup India
   https://www.startupindia.gov.in/
f. Many colleges today have an entrepreneurship cell
   and a way to connect with the larger ecosystem.

It takes a village to grow a start-up. Be fearless, connect with people, ask for help and march ahead!

#5
SIGNING OFF WITH A NOTE TO START OFF!

The start-up ecosystem around you will provide support, but the toughest battles will be fought inside your own head. You will question yourself frequently, doubt your decisions, feel dejected one day and elated the next. Sometimes your goals will seem like mountains that cannot be climbed. Don't ever think that you can't. Just think about what will help you do it. Focus on taking a step at a time, and eventually you will reach the peak you were eyeing! It will be a tough journey at times but will definitely prove to be rewarding. At times, some decisions will not work out the way

you would have planned. It's all right. Learn from it and do better next time.

There are inspiring stories of real entrepreneurs all around you. iD Fresh Food is a multi-crore business today across countries. Its founder comes from a humble background—he failed sixth grade and had to repeat the year, but he went on to become an engineer. He ran a small sweets shop as a ten-year-old to earn pocket money! He started iD Fresh Food with a capital of Rs 50,000 in 2005. In ten years, the company crossed Rs 100 crore in the annual **turnover**!

Look at another role model: Kiran Mazumdar-Shaw. She set up Biocon Ltd in 1978 when not many people believed in the business model or her ability as an entrepreneur. She started her company from a small garage and grew it to what is now a multibillion-dollar biotechnology firm.

Nothing is impossible. Any business idea can grow into a giant company. From several college dorm start-ups to many garage start-ups and even kitchen table start-ups that shaped the way we live today with their products and services, even the sky is not the limit for a determined entrepreneur!

Throughout this book, we have discussed examples of seemingly small businesses, such as lemonade and cupcakes, a neighbourhood reading club and website-building services. But no business is small when executed well. Think of a roadside chaiwallah— the same business got a makeover as Chai Point and Chaayos. Remember the humble sugar cane juice seller? The same business became as big as Cane Crush and Raw Pressery. Simple recipes of aamras and jaljeera, which one would easily make at home, transformed into Paper Boat. So why not lemonade or cupcakes? Neighbourhood reading sessions done as a podcast can become big. If you think about it innovatively and execute relentlessly, any business can become big.

So, what's going to be your big dream?

GLOSSARY

- **brand.** A unique combination of a name and associated logo used by a business as its mark to identify its products or services.
- **break-even point.** A point in business at which total revenue is equal to total expenses, thus resulting in no profit and no loss.
- **capital.** Money required to start or grow a business.
- **customer.** A person who buys and pays for the product or service offered by a business.
- **debt.** Loan, borrowed money on which typically a borrower has to pay interest.
- **direct cost.** Cost associated with material and labour that directly goes into a product. Total direct cost for a business increases with each unit produced.
- **expenses.** Money paid out for buying products and services.
- **founder.** A person who starts a new business.
- **indirect cost.** Cost associated with facilities, management and other activities that do not directly become part of the final product. Total

indirect cost for a business does not change much with each unit produced.

- **logistics.** A system through which products are transported and delivered to buyers.
- **logo.** A picture or symbol or artwork used by a business as its mark to identify its products or services.
- **margin.** The amount by which revenue exceeds expenses in a business.
- **markup.** The extra amount added to the cost to arrive at the selling price.
- **net profit.** Surplus of revenue after paying for all (direct plus indirect) costs.
- **operating profit.** Surplus of revenue after paying for direct costs.
- **revenue.** Income of a business.
- **selling price.** The price at which one unit of a product or service is sold by the company.
- **start-up incubators and accelerators.** Institutions that support early stage businesses and early entrepreneurs with ideas, with seed capital and with mentoring and technical advice.
- **strategy.** A plan of action designed to achieve the long-term objective.
- **turnover.** Revenue made by a business in a particular time period (usually a year).

ACKNOWLEDGEMENTS

It takes a village to bring out a book too! Many thanks to the wonderful and patient team at Penguin Random House India for giving the book the best possible shape and form. I am grateful to Sanjay Anandaram, a well-known investor, mentor and a passionate supporter of entrepreneurship, for reviewing an early draft of this book.

The contents of this book evolved from an actual programme run at a school. I can't thank Deepa Sridhar, the principal of Sri Kumarans Public School in Bangalore, enough—for being open-minded and giving an opportunity to run a one-of-a-kind programme. Thanks are due to the co-creator of this programme, Nikhil Gumbhir (we also co-wrote *Become a Junior Inventor*, which you must check out!) and my colleague Anuja Ranade who was an integral part of this journey.

Real learning comes from real life—mine came from my many entrepreneurial adventures. I thank my family and friends who stood by me through them all! Special thanks are due to the team and the wonderfully wise professors at IIM Bangalore and NS Raghavan Centre for Entrepreneurial Learning, as well as to many passionate entrepreneurs and mentors I met during my stint there, for shaping my thinking on the subject.

ABOUT VRUNDA BANSODE

Vrunda Bansode has over fifteen years of experience working across varied functions and domains in MNCs, start-ups and social sector organizations. She currently heads India Data Insights, a data portal for the Indian social sector, at Sattva Consulting. This book draws on her extensive experience in entrepreneurship development that comes from co-founding and running her own ventures, managing incubation programmes at IIM Bangalore and from the hands-on entrepreneurship lab she ran for high school students for five years. She holds a master's degree in commerce and economics from the University of Pune and a PGDMB from Indo-German Chamber of Commerce, Mumbai. She has previously co-authored the book *Become a Junior Inventor*.

READ MORE FROM THE SERIES

Become a Junior Inventor

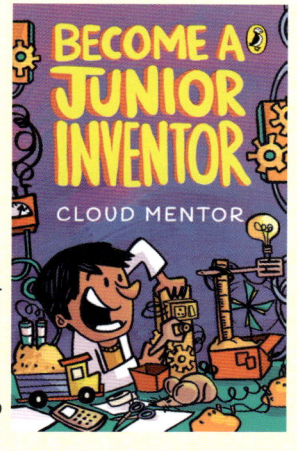

Ages 9 and up

Imagine, Invent, Engineer!

Ever wondered how roller coasters work? Been fascinated with solar panels and windmills, batteries and switches, wires and bulbs? Get acquainted with these movers and shakers of the world of gadgetry around us . . . and become a junior inventor yourself!

Written by Cloud Mentor, a company that mentors kids to become budding inventors, this fun book features almost every conceivable topic of interest—from machines and circuits to structural innovations and design basics. Learn how to make a waterwheel, create your own bottle boat at home and explore the science behind your favourite toy.